THE BELIEF DETOX

Stop Believing, Start Living

JULIE CLOUTIER

WEALTH ACTIVATOR

ISBN: 9798271557729

Published by JC, Wealth Activator

For inquiries, please contact: hello@juliecloutier.com

To Lambert, my partner of 25 years, who, in the midst of our shared struggles and limiting beliefs, asked me to seek the answers that would set us free. Because of his courage and curiosity, we've transformed pain into freedom, searched into love, and struggled into a life of joy, expansion, and continued growth.

CONTENTS

JULIE CLOUTIER

Introduction

WHAT IF EVERYTHING you've been taught to believe is upside down?

What if the very ideas you cling to—about who you are, what's possible, and how life "works"—are the chains keeping you from freedom?

The truth is, most of us don't live from Truth. We live from beliefs—assumptions we picked up from family, culture, society, and our past experiences. Some of these serve us. Many of them don't. They limit us, shrink us, and box us in. And because we've repeated them so often, they feel like reality.

But here's the secret: beliefs are not Truth. Beliefs are choices you continue to rehearse. They can be dropped, replaced, or completely dissolved the moment you see through them.

This book is not about working harder, hustling longer, or adding new strategies to your already crowded life. It's about *unsubscribing*—gently and radically letting go of the thought-patterns that sabotage you. When you do, you'll see how life naturally reorganizes itself with ease.

We'll focus on the three arenas where limiting beliefs run the deepest: **health, relationships, and money**. These are the mirrors that reflect back your inner world most clearly. Change the way you relate to them on the inside, and the outside cannot help but transform.

This book is an invitation to **question everything you think you know**. It's an invitation to explore the beliefs that shape your health, your relationships, your money, and the very thoughts that run your inner world.

When we carry limiting beliefs, our minds filter reality to find proof of them. We notice what's missing, what's wrong, what's impossible. But when we learn to **unsubscribe from these beliefs**, we begin to notice the inverse: abundance, vitality, love, and ease—all around us.

If you are ready to question everything you think you know, you're in the right place. If you are ready for radical change—not through force, but through release—this book is for you.

What This Book Offers

You will discover:

- How your **inner dialogue** shapes every choice, action, and outcome.
- How **limiting beliefs** about health, love, and money create struggle and scarcity.
- How to **notice abundance** and let it grow in your life.
- How to **embody gratitude**, amplifying joy and connection.
- How to **live the inverse**, aligning effortlessly with your true state of being.

This is not a book about strategies, hacks, or willpower. This is a book about **being differently**—about shifting the energy within, so your life naturally mirrors what you truly are.

Transformation happens not in doing more, but in **being differently, noticing differently, and trusting the abundance that already exists**.

If you are ready to question everything, to see life from a new perspective, and to step into a reality shaped by possibility instead of limitation, this book is for you.

Open your mind. Open your heart. And begin to **see the world, and yourself, anew**.

PART I

THE FOUNDATION

Chapter 1

What Are Beliefs?

MOST PEOPLE LIVE their entire lives inside invisible cages. They wake up, go to work, fall in love, raise families, earn money, and even grow old—all while assuming the bars of their cage are made of iron. But here's the truth: the bars aren't made of iron. They're made of thoughts.

A belief is not Truth.

A belief is simply a thought you've repeated enough times that it feels unquestionable.

Think about that for a moment.

Every story you tell yourself about who you are, what's possible for you, what you can have, what you can't have—every single one of those is a belief. You weren't born with them. You picked them up. You absorbed them from parents, teachers, culture, religion, media, friends, and from your own experiences. Over time, you kept rehearsing them until they became part of your identity.

But just because you've believed something for years doesn't make it true.

Beliefs vs. Truth

Here's the distinction most people never make:

- **Truth is what simply *is*.** It doesn't change. It doesn't depend on your opinion. It just *is*.
- **Belief is a filter.** It colours the way you see Truth. If your filter says, "Life is hard," you will experience life as hard. If your filter says, "Love always hurts," you will live inside that story.

Your beliefs don't reflect reality—they *create* the reality you experience.

How Beliefs Sneak In

Most limiting beliefs enter your life quietly. You don't choose them consciously.

- A parent sighs, "Money doesn't grow on trees."
- A teacher says, "Not everyone is cut out for success."
- A doctor shakes their head and tells you, "That's just what happens when you get older."

At first, these are just words. But if you hear them enough times—and especially if you hear them when you're young or vulnerable—they become instructions for how to live. They become your *rules for reality*.

You didn't create these beliefs, but you live by them as if they were law.

Why Questioning Beliefs Is So Powerful

Here's the radical shift: the moment you recognize a belief as a belief—not as Truth—you begin to loosen its grip.

It's like realizing you've been wearing tinted glasses your whole life. You thought the world was naturally gray. But no—the lens was gray. Take off the glasses, and suddenly the colours return.

When you begin questioning your beliefs, you step into the most powerful position a human can occupy: **choice.** You can keep the belief, drop it, or replace it with one that actually supports you.

A New Possibility

So let me ask you:

- What if the things you're most certain about are exactly what's holding you back?
- What if the very stories you defend are the ones creating your struggle?
- What if the opposite of what you believe is actually closer to Truth?

This book is not about adding more beliefs. It's about *subtracting the ones that never belonged to you in the first place.*

Because the lighter you travel, the freer you become.

Now that you've begun noticing the beliefs shaping your life, the next step is to see just how powerful they are. Beliefs don't just exist in your mind—they create the world you experience.

Reflection & Practice: Chapter 1: What are Beliefs?

These exercises are about **awareness and curiosity**. Nothing needs to change immediately—just noticing is the first step to freedom.

1. Spot Your Beliefs

Take a notebook and write down 3–5 beliefs that feel absolute in each area of your life:

- Health (e.g., "I'm just not energetic," "I always get sick in winter")
- Relationships (e.g., "People always leave," "I can't trust others")
- Money (e.g., "I'll never have enough," "Money is hard to get")

- Then ask: Where did this belief come from? Whose voice am I repeating?

2. **Question the Truth**

Pick one belief from above. Ask yourself:

- Is this absolutely true, or just something I've assumed?
- Can I think of even one situation where the opposite is true?
- Is it true for everyone all the time?
- How would I feel if I didn't hold this belief?

3. **Imagine the Opposite**

Take one limiting belief and flip it into its inverse. For example:

- "Life is hard." → "Life is easy."
- "I can't have financial freedom" → "Money flows to me with ease."
- Don't force belief—just imagine it as an experiment. Notice shifts in your energy, thoughts, or reactions. Connect to the emotion of how it would feel if it were true.

4. **Catch the Reflex**

For the next few days, pay attention to your inner talk. Every time a limiting thought arises, pause and say:

"This is a belief, not Truth."

Notice how simply recognizing it changes your energy and perspective.

5. Open the Door

Practice this simple invitation:

- "What if it is possible for me?"

Say it out loud. Let your body feel the openness and curiosity. Let this question guide your awareness throughout the book.

Chapter 2

The Power of Beliefs

EVERYTHING IN YOUR life begins in your mind.

The beliefs you hold—about yourself, about others, and about the world—shape every choice, every habit, and every experience.

Beliefs are like lenses. They filter reality, highlighting some things while obscuring others. When you hold limiting beliefs, your world reflects limitation. When you hold expansive beliefs, your world reflects possibility.

Beliefs Create Reality

Consider these examples:

- If you believe, *"I am always tired,"* you will notice fatigue more than energy, weakness more than strength, and illness more than vitality.
- If you believe, *"People don't value me,"* you will see rejection and indifference, while missing acts of love and appreciation.

- If you believe, *"I'll never have enough,"* scarcity will dominate your perception, even in moments of abundance.

Your brain is incredibly efficient at proving your beliefs. This is why the same person can experience the same situation entirely differently depending on the beliefs they hold.

Limiting Beliefs vs. Expansive Beliefs

A **limiting belief** is any thought that keeps you small, restricted, or stuck. Examples:

- "I'm not good enough."
- "Love is always hard."
- "Money doesn't grow on trees."

An **expansive belief** is a thought that frees you, opens possibilities, and aligns you with your true potential. Examples:

- "I am worthy of joy, love, and abundance."
- "Healthy, vibrant relationships flow to me naturally."
- "Abundance is everywhere, and I am connected to it."

The first step in transforming your life is noticing which beliefs dominate your inner world. Once you see them, you can begin to **unsubscribe from the limiting ones** and **embody the expansive ones**.

The Cycle of Proof

Limiting beliefs are self-reinforcing. They create a loop:

1. You hold a belief.
2. Your brain filters reality to find proof of it.
3. The evidence reinforces the belief.
4. The cycle repeats.

Example: You believe, *"People never invite me to anything."*

- You notice only the invitations you didn't receive.
- You ignore invitations or gestures of connection.
- The belief strengthens.

Breaking this cycle requires conscious awareness. Once you do, your inner world shifts—and your outer reality begins to mirror it.

Freedom in Unsubscribing

The moment you realize that beliefs are **not the absolute truth**, you gain freedom.

- Not all thoughts are facts.
- Not all assumptions are reality.
- You can choose which beliefs to keep and which to release.

This book is your guide to:

- Seeing where your beliefs have been limiting you.
- Learning to unsubscribe from what no longer serves you.
- Noticing the proof of the inverse, abundance, and possibility.
- Living a life shaped by conscious choice rather than unconscious belief.

Awareness alone is powerful, but awareness plus action is transformative. In Chapter 3, we'll practice the art of unsubscribing—letting go of limiting beliefs so that your life can shift effortlessly.

Reflection & Practice: Chapter 2: The Power of Beliefs

These exercises are about **awareness, noticing patterns, and experimenting with perspective**. The goal is not effort—it's observation.

1. **Spot the Inherited Beliefs**

Take your notebook and reflect on what you heard most often growing up:

- Health (e.g., "illness runs in our family," "aging means decline")
- Relationships (e.g., "love always fades," "people can't be trusted")

- Money (e.g., "rich people are greedy," "money is hard to come by")
- Ask: Whose voice do these beliefs actually belong to—mine, or someone else's?

2. Separate Belief from Truth

Choose one belief you wrote down. Ask yourself:

- Is this absolutely true, or just something I assumed?
- Can I think of even one example where the opposite is true?
- How does my life look when I believe this thought?
- How would life look if I no longer believed it?

3. The Inverse Experiment

Take one limiting belief and flip it into its opposite. For example:

- "Life is hard" → "Life is easy"
- "I always struggle with money" → "Money flows to me with ease"
- Don't force belief—just imagine the opposite for 24 hours. Notice shifts in energy, decisions, or responses from others.

4. **Catch the Whisper**

For the next week, observe your inner talk. Each time you hear a limiting story ("I can't," "I'm not good enough," "This never works for me"), pause and say:

- "That's a belief, not Truth."
- Awareness is the first crack in the cage of limitation.

5. **Notice the Evidence**

Consciously look for moments that support the opposite of your limiting belief. For example, if you usually notice scarcity, notice abundance instead. Record these observations—small proofs accumulate and begin to shift your perception.

Chapter 3

Unsubscribe: Step Into Freedom

WHAT IF THE VERY thoughts you've been battling are the ones holding you back?

Most people think change is about adding more. More affirmations. More strategies. More hustle. More rituals. More doing.

But the truth is, transformation doesn't come from stacking more beliefs on top of the ones already weighing you down. Transformation comes from subtraction. From release. From the simple act of unsubscribing.

The Trap of Self-Improvement

Look around—an entire industry tells you that you're broken and must be fixed, or healed: books, courses, podcasts, coaching programs.

But the truth? You were never broken. What weighs you down isn't you—it's what you've been carrying.

Trying to fix yourself is like rearranging furniture in a burning house. You're busy. You're working. But the fire—your limiting beliefs—still rages on.

Unsubscribing is different. It's stepping out of the fire entirely.

What Does It Mean to Unsubscribe?

To unsubscribe means to stop buying into the thought-patterns that don't serve you.

It means recognizing: *this is just a belief, not Truth*—and then consciously choosing to let it go.

Think of your mind like an inbox. Every day, hundreds of messages—beliefs, opinions, stories—arrive. Some are useful. Many are spam. You don't need to read every spam email. You don't need to argue with it. You don't even need to mark it as important. You simply click unsubscribe.

You stop feeding it your attention. And when you stop subscribing to limiting beliefs, they stop shaping your reality.

Why Unsubscribing Works Effortlessly

Fighting beliefs takes effort—you push, affirm, struggle to "make yourself believe" something new. Many burn out trying to swim upstream.

Unsubscribing is different: no struggle, no force. You simply release what was never yours. Change becomes effortless. You're not carrying extra weight anymore.

The Inverse of Fixing: Returning

The moment you let go of a false belief, you don't need to replace it with anything.

The Truth naturally reveals itself.

- Drop the belief that "health declines with age," and you return to a sense of vitality.
- Drop the belief that "love always hurts," and you return to openness.
- Drop the belief that "money is scarce," and you return to abundance.

You're not adding something new—you're returning to what has always been available.

A Radical Choice

Unsubscribing isn't complicated. It's a choice.

- The choice to no longer entertain what isn't serving you.
- The choice to walk away from thoughts that keep you small.
- The choice to stop fixing—and start freeing.

This chapter isn't here to convince you. It's here to remind you: you always have the power to unsubscribe.

Reflection & Practice: Chapter 3: Unsubscribe: Step into Freedom

1. Your Mental Inbox

Imagine your mind as an email inbox. For the next day, notice every "belief notification" that pops up. When you catch a thought like, "I can't do this" or "This is just the way life is," pause and say:

- "This is spam. I unsubscribe."
- Write down at least three beliefs you "unsubscribed" from during the day.

2. The Effort Test

Think of a belief you've been trying really hard to overcome (e.g., "I'll never find love," "I'm not good with money"). Ask yourself:

- How much effort has this belief cost me?
- What would it feel like if I simply stopped giving it attention?

Close your eyes and imagine walking away from this belief like you're walking out of a burning house. Describe that feeling in one sentence.

3. Practice Unsubscribing

Reclaim your focus and energy. Every time you consciously unsubscribe from a thought, habit, or expectation, you create space for what truly nourishes you:

- **Identify the Noise:** Take 5 minutes to write down three beliefs, habits, or expectations that no longer feel aligned (e.g., "I must always be available," "I can't rest until everything is done," "Success means struggle").
- **Practice the Unsubscribe Statement:** For each item, say out loud:

  "I unsubscribe from this belief."

  Repeat until you feel a shift—however small—in your body or energy.

4. Replace with Truth

Choose one belief you just released and write down a supportive alternative. Example:

- "I must always be available." → "It is safe to rest. My worth is not measured by constant doing or always being available for others."
- **Daily Scan:** For the next week, when you notice yourself reacting out of habit or obligation,

pause and silently say: *Unsubscribe.* Notice how your body softens when you choose differently.

5. Evidence of Freedom

Begin noticing moments that reflect the **inverse of the beliefs you unsubscribed from**. For instance, if you released "I am not seen or heard," notice gestures of kindness or connection. Record them. Seeing the inverse reinforces the freedom you are creating.

Remember: every time you unsubscribe, you reclaim space for your true life. By clearing the noise, you open room for clarity, alignment, and ease.

PART II

THE THREE ARENAS

Chapter 4

Health

MANY PEOPLE BELIEVE their body is their enemy.

They live in constant battle with it—criticizing its shape, resenting its pain, distrusting its signals. Some treat health like a fragile thing, easily broken, always slipping away.

But what if the opposite is true?

What if your body is not betraying you at all, but faithfully mirroring your beliefs back to you?

The Belief–Body Connection

Your body listens to your inner talk more than it listens to your doctor, your diet, or your workout plan. Every thought you repeat becomes a subtle instruction to your cells.

- Believe that "aging means decline," and you'll notice every wrinkle, every ache, every limitation as proof.

- Believe that "illness runs in my family," and your body will quietly organize itself to match that story.
- Believe that "I don't have time for health," and your body will comply by draining your energy.

This isn't magic—it's alignment. Your body follows the path your beliefs lay out.

The Inverse of Illness

Consider this: what if sickness is not the default, but health is?

Think about a cut on your skin. Without any effort from you, the body repairs itself. Cells multiply.

Tissue knits together. A new layer forms. Your body doesn't ask your permission—it simply knows how to heal.

Now imagine if that same intelligence is always working, in every organ, every system, every moment.

The only thing that interrupts this flow? Beliefs that say it's not possible.

Why Diets, Routines, and Fixes Don't Stick

How many people do you know who start a new health regimen with full enthusiasm, only to drop it weeks later?

The reason isn't a lack of willpower. It's because the underlying belief never changed.

- If you secretly believe "I'll always be tired," no supplement will keep you energized for long.
- If you believe "I'm destined to struggle with my weight," no program will bring lasting ease.
- If you believe "my body is against me," every effort will feel like pushing uphill.

Until the belief shifts, the body must keep fulfilling the script it's been given.

A New Way to See Health

Health is not something you earn. Health is your natural state.

When you unsubscribe from the belief that your body is fragile, broken, or doomed, you return to the truth: vitality is your baseline.

Imagine speaking to your body as an ally instead of an enemy:

- "My body knows how to heal."
- "Energy is natural for me."
- "I trust my body to do what it was designed to do."

The body responds not to punishment, but to partnership.

The Invitation

Instead of fighting your body into submission, begin noticing the beliefs that shape your relationship with it. Ask yourself:

- What stories have I inherited about health?
- Do these stories empower me, or weaken me?
- Am I willing to unsubscribe from the ones that keep me sick, tired, or afraid?

Reflection & Practice: Chapter 4: Health

Your body is a mirror, reflecting the stories you've been carrying. These exercises are about listening, not controlling.

1. **Uncover the Story**

   Write down the first five automatic thoughts about your body or health. Notice them without editing.

2. **Trace the Source**

   Ask: Where did I learn this? Family, culture, media, or past experiences? Recognize whose story you've been repeating.

3. **Flip the Script**

   Choose one limiting thought and try its opposite.

Example: "My body always betrays me" → "My body is on my side."

Say it aloud and notice how your body responds. If your body contracts with the new belief, simply notice where the sensation is arising.

Stay with the sensation, focus your awareness on the sensation, making it bigger and bigger. Simply staying with the body sensation, making it bigger, can have a powerful effect, where the sensation grows so much that it completely expands in the space/dissipates.

Once the sensation has dissipated, do it again, repeat the affirmation, feel your body sensation, make it bigger until it expands so much it dissipates.

By the third time, the sensation will probably feel smaller until, by the fourth or fifth time, your body will feel open and expanded with the statement.

4. **Affirmation of Safety**

Place a hand on your heart and say: "It is safe to trust my body. My body and I are on the same team."

Chapter 5

Relationships

MANY PEOPLE BELIEVE that love is something you have to chase, earn, or negotiate.

They live in a world of "not enough": not enough affection, not enough attention, not enough loyalty. They assume that relationships are hard, painful, and never quite satisfying.

But what if the opposite is true?

What if the quality of your relationships is a reflection of the beliefs you hold about love, connection, and your own worth?

The Belief–Relationship Connection

Every pattern in your relationships—romantic, familial, or professional—starts with a thought you hold about yourself.

- Believe that "I am unlovable," and people will unconsciously mirror that back.

- Believe that "Everyone eventually hurts me," and you'll attract conflict and disappointment.
- Believe that "I don't deserve closeness" and distance will dominate your relationships.
- Believe that "People don't like having me around," and your brain will find evidence of that to reinforce the belief. You'll even unconsciously create circumstances producing that very outcome that proves your belief.

Your inner world creates your outer world. The quality of love you experience is a direct reflection of how you relate to yourself.

The Inverse of Lack

Consider this: the universe doesn't withhold love. Love is abundant.

The challenge isn't finding it—it's recognizing it.

When you stop believing in scarcity and unworthiness, you stop chasing. You stop settling. You stop contracting in fear. And the people, connections, and intimacy you truly desire begin to appear naturally.

Why Relationships Repeat Patterns

Many people complain that "history repeats itself" in relationships. Same fights, same heartbreak, same disappointment.

It's not because the world is unfair—it's because your beliefs are running the script. Until the inner story changes, the outer experience cannot change.

- If you believe "I will always be rejected," you might unconsciously push people away.
- If you believe "I can't trust anyone," you might notice only the behaviours that confirm it.
- If you believe "Love is painful," you might unknowingly recreate the drama you expect.

Until you unsubscribe from these beliefs, relationships will continue to mirror them.

A New Way to See Love

What if you treated yourself as the person you've been seeking?

- Believe in your own worthiness, and others will recognize it.
- Believe in abundance, and scarcity will lose its grip.
- Believe in trust, and fear will loosen.

Love does not have to be complicated. It simply asks: *Do you believe you are enough? Do I realize that the world sees me as I see me?*

The Invitation

Examine your closest relationships. Ask yourself:

- Which beliefs about love have I been carrying?
- How have these beliefs shaped my experiences?
- Am I willing to unsubscribe from the beliefs that limit connection and closeness?

Because love flows effortlessly to those who stop resisting it from within.

Reflection & Practice: Chapter 5: Relationships

1. **Identify Your Relationship Scripts**

Journal: What messages about love or connection did I hear growing up? Which do I still carry?

2. **Catch the Pattern**

Identify a recurring issue. Ask: What belief about love drives this pattern? How has it shaped my experience?

3. **Flip the Story**

Choose one limiting belief and invert it:

"Something is wrong with me." → "I am worthy of love and connection."

Notice changes in interactions and feelings for one week.

4. **Practice Self-Worth Daily**

Each morning, place a hand on your heart: "I am worthy of love. I am open to connection. I trust the flow of relationships."

5. **Reflection Journal Prompt**

End of week: Which belief was easiest to release? Which still lingers? How have my relationships shifted?

Chapter 6

Money

MANY PEOPLE BELIEVE that money is hard to come by, that wealth is reserved for a few, and that financial security is a constant struggle.

They stress, save, hustle, and worry—all while feeling like they're never enough.

But what if the opposite is true?

What if money is abundant, and your relationship with it reflects your inner beliefs more than your external circumstances?

The Belief–Money Connection

Every financial pattern in your life—scarcity, stress, abundance, or ease—starts with a thought you hold about yourself and about money.

- Believe that "I'll never be wealthy," and opportunities may pass you by unnoticed.

- Believe that "I don't deserve financial freedom," and you may unconsciously sabotage your income.
- Believe that "money is evil and is the source of suffering," and you may repel it even while pursuing it.

Your inner conversation about money creates the reality you experience. Change the conversation, and the flow of money changes too.

The Inverse of Scarcity

Consider this: the universe doesn't ration wealth. Money is energy, constantly moving, constantly available.

The challenge isn't scarcity—it's your perception.

- If you see limits, your life will conform to limits.
- If you see abundance, your life will begin to reflect abundance.

Money is a mirror. It reflects the beliefs you hold about value, worthiness, and possibility.

Why Struggle Feels Necessary

Many people believe that financial success must be hard-earned, that sacrifice is proof of worth, and that comfort is impossible without struggle.

But these beliefs are optional. They are stories, not laws.

- Working long hours while feeling trapped? That may reflect a belief that "I can't earn easily."
- Stressing about bills constantly? That may reflect a belief that "I will always be lacking or I am running out of money."
- Obsessively comparing yourself to others? That may reflect a belief that "I am not enough."

Until the underlying story changes, struggle is inevitable—because your life is always following the script of your beliefs.

A New Way to See Money

What if you treated money like a loyal partner, rather than a scarce resource?

- Believe in your own worth, and money will follow.
- Believe in abundance, and opportunities appear where none seemed to exist.
- Believe in ease, and financial flow becomes natural.

Money is not about pushing, controlling, or fearing—it's about aligning your inner story with the reality you want.

The Invitation

Look honestly at your financial beliefs:

- Which inherited or personal beliefs about money are still running my life?
- How have these beliefs shaped my income, spending, and sense of security?
- Am I willing to unsubscribe from scarcity, fear, and self-doubt?

Because when you release limiting beliefs about money, wealth stops being a struggle and becomes a natural expression of your energy.

Reflection & Practice: Chapter 6: Money

1. Your Money Story

Journal three beliefs you grew up noticing about money. For example:

- o "Money doesn't grow on trees."
- o "You must work hard to deserve it."
- o "Rich people are selfish or dishonest."

2. Inherited or Chosen?

Ask: Whose belief is this—parent, teacher, society, or my own?

3. **The Scarcity Filter**

For one day, notice every "not enough" thought. Pause and say: *"That's a belief, not Truth."*

4. **Flip into the Story**

Choose one scarcity thought and invert it:

"There's never enough." → "There is more than enough" OR "I always have what I need now and a little bit more."

Live from this for 24 hours and notice shifts.

5. **Proof of Abundance**

Look around your home. Name five objects that show abundance aloud (chair, phone, food, etc.).

6. **Practice The Recognition of Having Enough**

Any time you interact with money, spending or paying bills, pause and tell yourself, I am grateful that I have money to pay this. This will short-circuit the voice in the background that might be saying, "I am running out of money."

PART III

INTEGRATION

Chapter 7

Assumptions: The Invisible Architecture of Reality

MANY PEOPLE THINK they live from truth.

But no one lives from truth. We live from **assumptions**.

An assumption is a quiet agreement you've made with reality. It's the lens through which you interpret, react, and create. It colors every decision, every emotion, every result.

You don't attract what you want.

You attract what you *assume* to be yours.

If you assume that life is hard, it will mirror back difficulty.

If you assume that people can't be trusted, you'll keep meeting those who prove it.

If you assume that money is scarce, you'll keep finding yourself right.

Your world doesn't contradict your assumptions — it *echoes* them.

The Echo

Life is always responding, not to your words, but to your inner certainty.

The tone of your energy sets the tone of your experience.

Every conversation, every delay, every opportunity carries your assumptions within it.

The echo is not personal — it's precise.

Reality mirrors your inner world with exact accuracy, not to punish you, but to *reveal you to yourself.*

When you change the assumption, the echo changes automatically.

It's not about effort — it's about alignment.

The Sleep of Inherited Thought

Most assumptions aren't consciously chosen — they're absorbed.

We inherit them from our parents, our culture, our past.

We gather evidence for them so efficiently that they begin to feel like the truth.

That's how we fall asleep to our own power.

We forget that assumptions are not facts; they're *permissions.*

They dictate how far we let life go in our favor.

They define what we consider possible, available, or meant for us.

The more unaware you are of your assumptions, the more they define you.

The moment you become aware of them, they begin to dissolve.

Awareness: The Light That Ends the Spell

Awareness is liberation.

You cannot shift what you cannot see.

When you bring awareness to an assumption, you reclaim choice.

You see that nothing is "just the way it is."

Everything is responding to the way you *see* it.

Awareness doesn't fight the old pattern — it ends the illusion of its power.

You don't have to fix the assumption. You only have to *see* it clearly.

Seeing it fully is enough to make it lose its hold.

The Body: Your First Language of Truth

Here's what most people miss:

When you shift an assumption, your **body** will tell you if it's true for you.

If the new belief feels like tension, resistance, or collapse in your body, it's not integrated yet. It's still mental — an idea sitting on top of an old vibration.

You can't override the body and call it alignment.

You can't affirm yourself into coherence.

Your body is the tuning fork of your truth.

It knows before the mind does.

It feels the difference between what's conceptually beautiful and what's energetically real.

Every time you claim a new assumption — "I am fully supported," "Money flows with ease," "Love is safe for me" — pause.

Breathe.

Let the breath travel through your whole body, as if you're *inhaling the new code into your cells.*

Allow the breath to soften the resistance and create spaciousness.

With each exhale, feel your body *dropping the new code* deeper — as if it's reprogramming your nervous system to feel safe inside this new truth.

your body doesn't feel open, don't force it.

vith it. Let it show you where the old assumption

That's the place where awareness becomes embodiment.

Transformation happens when your *nervous system agrees* with your new truth.

Without that agreement, the shift stays surface-level — an intellectual upgrade that never roots into your reality.

So before you try to "believe harder," come home to your body.

Let it tell you what's still unhealed.

Let it guide you to safety, openness, and coherence.

Because when the body relaxes, life begins to respond differently — instantly

The Invitation

Start to notice the quiet sentences running your life:

"People are too busy for me."

"Things take me longer."

"Good things never last."

"I always have to do it alone."

Each one is a portal.

You can keep rehearsing it, or you can unsubscribe.

Pause.

Breathe.

Choose again.

"Life responds to my openness."

"Things work out beautifully for me."

"Good things are meant to last."

"I am supported in ways I cannot yet see.

Reflection & Practice: Chapter 7: Assumptions: The Invisible Architecture of Reality

1. Catch the Whisper.

Notice your inner commentary throughout the day — the subtle predictions, the quiet doubts. Those are assumptions revealing themselves.

2. Name the Echo.

Where has this assumption already shaped your life? Notice the pattern it's been repeating.

3. Feel the Body.

Say your new assumption out loud and notice your body's reaction. If it tightens, meet that resistance with compassion — not correction. Presence is what makes the body feel safe to believe.

4. Breathe in the New Code.

Take a slow, conscious breath as you repeat your new assumption. Imagine breathing this new frequency into your heart, your belly, your cells. Feel your body *dropping the code in*, layer by layer.

Let your breath carry the new assumption from concept to embodiment — until the body feels a subtle sigh of *yes*.

5. Live the New Certainty.

Move through your day as though this new assumption is already your baseline. Not as performance, but as coherence. Watch as reality mirrors the inner safety of your new state.

Assumptions are the architecture of your reality.

They determine what you expect, and what you expect becomes what you experience.

Awareness opens the structure.

The body stabilizes it.

Breath anchors it.

When mind, body, and breath agree, manifestation becomes effortless — not because you're forcing it, but because you're finally resonating with it.

Life is not showing you what's real.

Life is showing you what you *believe* is real.

And your body always knows the difference.

Chapter 8

The Practice of Inner Talk

MOST PEOPLE THINK change happens when they *do more.*

Eat better, work harder, save more, love more… But real transformation doesn't start in the external world. It starts in your inner world—with your thoughts, your inner talk, and the beliefs you allow to run on autopilot.

Your inner dialogue is the engine driving every choice, habit, and experience in life. Change the conversation inside, and the world outside begins to shift effortlessly.

Why Inner Talk Matters

Every belief you've held about health, love, or money lives in your inner conversation.

- The words you whisper to yourself shape your self-esteem.

- The stories you repeat determine the relationships you attract.
- The narratives you carry influence how wealth flows into your life.

If you listen closely, you'll notice: most inner talk is automatic, reactive, and often negative. It's a loop of limiting beliefs you've rehearsed for years.

Changing your life doesn't start by changing circumstances. It starts by noticing and reshaping that loop.

The Three Steps of Inner Talk

1. Awareness

First, notice the thoughts you're telling yourself.

- "I'm too tired to exercise."
- "I'll never find love."
- "I can't earn more money."

Awareness is the key. You cannot change what you cannot see.

2. Interruption

The moment you catch a limiting thought, pause. Interrupt the loop.

- Say to yourself: *"This is a belief, not Truth."*
- Take a breath, smile, and step back.

Interrupting doesn't mean forcing positivity. It means recognizing that you don't have to obey every thought.

3. Reframe or Release

Finally, choose to either reframe the thought or release it completely.

- Reframe: *"I am capable and I trust myself."*
- Release: Simply notice the thought, let it drift away, and return to presence.

The goal is not to fill your mind with perfect affirmations. The goal is freedom from thoughts that limit your life.

Making Inner Talk a Daily Practice

- **Morning Check-in:** Take 5 minutes each morning to notice the first thoughts that arise.
- **Midday Pause:** Catch automatic thoughts as they happen—use the interruption step.
- **Evening Reflection:** Journal any limiting beliefs you noticed and what you did to reframe or release them.

Consistency matters more than perfection. Over time, your inner conversation will shift, and the results will appear effortlessly in your health, relationships, and finances.

The Invitation

Your inner talk is your most loyal mirror. The moment you take responsibility for it, you reclaim your power.

Ask yourself daily:

- Which thought patterns am I unconsciously repeating?
- Which ones serve me, and which ones limit me?
- Am I willing to practice awareness, interruption, and release every day?

Mastering inner talk is the foundation for living a life aligned with Truth, free from the beliefs that have held you back.

Reflection & Practice: Chapter 8: The Practice of Inner Talk

Your inner talk is the constant background music of your life. By becoming conscious of it, you can choose the soundtrack that aligns with abundance, vitality, and love.

1. **Daily Awareness Journal**

For the next three days, jot down phrases you catch yourself repeating internally. Notice especially moments of:

- Self-doubt ("I can't," "I'm not enough")
- Scarcity ("There's not enough time/money")

- Fear of rejection ("They won't like me," "I'll be judged")

2. **Pause & Replace**

Each time you catch a limiting phrase, pause and say aloud or silently: *"This is just a belief, not Truth."*

Then gently replace it with the inverse.

Example: "I never get what I want" → "Life supports me."

3. **Morning Mantra**

Each morning, choose one empowering phrase that feels expansive. Examples:

- "My body is vibrant and alive."
- "I am worthy of love exactly as I am."
- "Money flows to me in expected and unexpected ways."

Repeat it 3 times with presence before you start your day.

4. **Embodied Inner Talk**

Say your chosen mantra out loud while standing tall, shoulders open, breathing deeply. Let your body *feel* the truth of the words. This helps anchor the new belief more deeply than words alone.

5. Evening Check-In

Before bed, write down one moment where your inner talk supported you positively that day. Celebrate it — no matter how small.

6. Affirmation of Power

Repeat daily: "My inner talk shapes my reality. I choose words that expand me, not limit me."

As you begin practicing inner talk with awareness, you'll see how quickly your reality shifts. Your words are not empty — they are seeds. Plant consciously, and watch the garden of your life transform.

Chapter 9

Living the Inverse of Limiting Beliefs

UP TO THIS POINT, we've explored how beliefs—and the assumptions beneath them—shape your health, relationships, and money. We've also seen how your inner talk either reinforces those assumptions or liberates you from them.

But awareness is the bridge. The moment you bring awareness to your body—the tension, the openness, the subtle cues—you begin to see which assumptions your body still holds. Because the body never lies. It reveals whether a new assumption has truly integrated or if it's still just circulating in the mind.

Now comes the most exciting step: living as if the inverse of your limiting beliefs is already true, which in fact it is already true.

This isn't about forcing change or pretending. It's about embodying the energy of freedom, abundance, and possibility. When you do, life aligns—naturally and effortlessly.

What Does Living the Inverse Look Like?

Living the inverse means:

- Seeing health as vitality, not struggle.
- Experiencing love as abundant, not scarce.
- Treating money as flowing energy, not a source of stress.

It's not a checklist—it's a state of being. Your thoughts, actions, and choices all begin to flow from this new alignment.

Example: Health

Instead of believing, *"I'll always feel tired and get sick,"* you live with the assumption that your body is capable, resilient, and naturally aligned with vitality.

- You make choices that feel energizing.
- You notice your body responding positively without force.
- Health becomes effortless rather than a constant struggle.

Example: Relationships

Instead of believing, *"Love always ends in pain,"* you embody worthiness and openness.

- You attract people who match your energy.
- Boundaries feel natural, not defensive.
- Connections are easier and more joyful.

Example: Money

Instead of believing, *"I'll never have enough,"* you align with abundance.

- Opportunities appear organically.
- Decisions feel confident and empowered.
- Financial flow becomes a reflection of your inner state.

The Energy of the Inverse

Living the inverse is about **energy, not effort**.

- You're not forcing outcomes.
- You're not chasing goals through struggle.
- You're simply inhabiting the state of being that already attracts what you desire.

When your inner world aligns with Truth, the outer world mirrors it effortlessly.

Integration in Daily Life

1. **Morning Alignment:** Begin each day by embodying your inverse beliefs.
    - *"I am vibrant, I am worthy, abundance flows to me."*
    - *Connect with your body while affirming.*
    - *If your body feels contracted, allow yourself to focus on the sensation and expand it. Make it bigger and bigger and watch as it expands infinitely and dissipates in space.*

This exercise is crucial to allow your body to open to the new expansive belief. So that this exercise is not only a mental exercise.

2. **Awareness Throughout the Day:** Notice when old limiting beliefs arise and gently unsubscribe.
3. **Evening Reflection:** Observe how living from the inverse shaped your experiences. Find proof of your new belief.

Over time, living the inverse becomes second nature. Your life begins to feel effortless, expansive, and aligned with your heart and true desires.

The Invitation

Ask yourself:

- Which limiting beliefs am I ready to fully release?
- How will I embody the inverse in my health, relationships, and money starting today?
- What would life feel like if I truly lived from the state of being I've been seeking?

Living the inverse is not a distant goal. It is **available to you right now**.

Reflection & Practice: Chapter 9: Living the Inverse of Limiting Beliefs

This chapter is about more than thinking differently — it's about *living* differently. To live the inverse means to embody the opposite of your limiting beliefs in real time, so that new evidence begins to appear all around you.

1. Identify Your Key Limiting Beliefs

Take a notebook and list your most persistent limiting beliefs in each area:

- **Health:** e.g., "I always feel tired," "I'm prone to illness."
- **Relationships:** e.g., "Love always ends in pain," "I'm unlovable."

- **Money:** e.g., "I'll never have enough," "I don't deserve wealth."

2. Flip Each Belief

For each limiting belief, write its inverse (opposite statement).

- Example: "I always feel tired" → "I am naturally energized and vital."
- Example: "Love always ends in pain" → "I attract love that is nurturing and abundant."
- Example: "I'll never have enough" → "Money flows to me with ease and abundance."

Read each inverse statement aloud and feel it in your body as if it's already true. Again, if your body contracts, repeat the exercise of making the sensation bigger and bigger. Your body will get used to the new statement. When it stays open with the statement, you have shifted the energy.

3. Daily Embodiment Exercise

Choose one inverse belief per day:

- Morning: Repeat it aloud or write it in your journal.
- Throughout the day: Notice your thoughts and gently return to the inverse whenever the old limiting thought arises.

- Evening: Reflect on any moments when living from the inverse changed your choices, feelings, or interactions.

4. Integration Checkpoints

At the end of the week, reflect:

- Which inverse belief felt easiest to embody?
- Which one requires more attention or release?
- What shifts did I notice in my energy, actions, and external experiences?
- How has living from the inverse influenced my health, relationships, or finances?

5. Create a "Living the Inverse" Ritual

Design a small daily ritual to anchor this practice:

- Light a candle or take a few deep breaths.
- Speak aloud your three key inverse beliefs (one per area).
- Visualize your life as if these truths are fully real and present, and feel your body. Does it feel open and expansive or not? If not, focus on the body sensation and make the sensation bigger and bigger. It might expand to a point where it dissipates. Because everything we focus on grows. Once the body accepts the new belief, it has to manifest more and more in your life.

This ritual reinforces the state of being and gradually rewires your inner landscape to naturally attract aligned experiences.

Chapter 10

Noticing Abundance

MOST PEOPLE LOOK AT life through a lens of lack.

- *"I never have enough energy."*
- *"No one ever appreciates me."*
- *"Money is always scarce."*

This isn't reality—it's the filter of your limiting beliefs. When you assume scarcity, your brain scans the world for proof, and you find exactly what you expect. Your mind is brilliant at confirming your beliefs. This is proven by science; it is called the reticular activation system (RAS).

But what if you consciously looked for the opposite? What if you trained yourself to notice abundance? Suddenly, the world begins to feel full, generous, and alive.

Health: Your Body as a Miracle

Your body is performing miracles every second.

- Your heart beats without conscious effort.
- Your lungs expand and contract effortlessly.
- Cells regenerate, injuries heal, and your body balances itself perfectly.

When you focus only on fatigue, illness, or what's "wrong," your brain filters out all this abundance. But when you consciously notice it, you begin to see the proof everywhere.

- You take a breath and feel vitality.
- You notice the intelligence of your body functioning effortlessly.
- You realize that even simple movement is evidence of abundance.

Abundance of health is always present—it was there even when you didn't see it.

Relationships: Love and Connection Everywhere

Relationships are full of abundance, too. Love and appreciation are constantly circulating around you.

- Your friends invite you, support you, and show up in small ways.
- Your partner expresses love, gratitude, and care in ways you might have overlooked.
- You express love, appreciation, and gratitude to those around you.

- Every interaction is an opportunity to give and receive love freely.

When you unconsciously believe, "*No one ever appreciates me,*" your brain filters the world to notice only lack. But when you shift your inner dialogue to "*Love and appreciation are everywhere,*" suddenly invitations, acts of kindness, and moments of connection become visible. You find proof of abundance, and more continues to appear.

Money: Seeing Wealth Already Present

Abundance is not somewhere in the future—it is already here. Look around:

- The objects you own, the food you eat, the technology you use—they are all forms of abundance.
- Opportunities, resources, and ideas are constantly available if you notice them.
- It's possible to feel gratitude when paying for something, gratitude about having access to resources that are enabling me to pay, even if that resource is a credit card.
- When you focus on scarcity, you miss this proof entirely.

As you unsubscribe from limiting beliefs about money, your perception shifts. You start noticing what's available. You realize that financial energy flows freely, and you are always connected to it.

The Filter of Limiting Beliefs

Here's the key: your brain is a filter.

- If you believe, *"People never invite me anywhere,"* you will only notice rejection.
- If you believe, *"I am always sick or tired,"* you will notice every ache and fatigue.
- If you believe, *"I'll never have enough,"* scarcity dominates your perception.

When you consciously unsubscribe from these beliefs and begin noticing the inverse, your brain starts finding proof of the new story. The more you look, the more you see, and abundance becomes undeniable.

Practicing the Shift

1. **Daily Abundance Scan**

   Take a moment each day to notice:

   - Health: your body breathing, moving, healing.
   - Relationships: expressions of love, appreciation, and connection.

- o Money: the abundance surrounding you in objects, opportunities, and resources.

2. **Internal Dialogue**

Replace, "I lack…" with, "Abundance is present and growing."

3. **Notice the Proof**

   Each time you see evidence of abundance, pause and acknowledge it. Let it reinforce the new belief.

4. **Trust the Flow**

   The more you notice, the more your life aligns with the abundance you've chosen to see. The universe mirrors your inner state, offering ever more proof of the inverse.

Abundance isn't rare. It's always here. Your limiting beliefs filtered it out—but now, when you consciously open your eyes and mind, the proof of abundance appears everywhere—health, love, money, and life itself.

Reflection & Practice: Chapter 10: Noticing Abundance

1. Daily Abundance Scan

Each morning or evening, take 5 minutes to consciously notice abundance in three areas:

Health:

- o Feel your body breathing, moving, and functioning effortlessly.
- o Notice any small acts of self-healing or vitality.

Relationships:

- o Observe gestures of love, appreciation, or connection from friends, family, or your partner.
- o Notice moments where you give love or appreciation freely without losing anything.

Money:

- o Take note of the abundance already around you—objects, opportunities, resources, and conveniences.
- o Recognize how wealth and energy are flowing through your life in small ways.

Write down at least 3 examples per category each day.

2. Catch the Filter

Throughout your day, notice when your mind defaults to lack:

- o "I never have enough energy."
- o "No one ever invites me."
- o "Money is always scarce."

Pause, and consciously reframe:

- *"Abundance is present and growing. I notice it now."*

3. Proof Journal

Each night, journal moments that serve as proof of abundance:

- Health: a body function, a surge of energy, or effortless movement.
- Relationships: a kind word, an invitation, or shared laughter.
- Money: recognize every time you interact/exchange with money that you have money in that moment. Journal your gratitude to pay, when you pay for something, noticing how much gratitude you have to be able to pay.

Over time, you will start to notice more and more evidence that aligns with your new inner story.

4. Abundance Meditation

Take 3–5 minutes to close your eyes and breathe:

- Visualize your body full of vitality.
- Imagine the love and appreciation circulating around you.
- See money and resources flowing easily in your life.

Repeat silently:

- *"Abundance is everywhere. I see it, I feel it, I am aligned with it."*

5. Weekly Reflection Prompt

At the end of the week, reflect:

- What abundance did I notice that I previously overlooked?
- How did focusing on abundance shift my energy, actions, or perceptions?
- Which area (health, relationships, money) felt easiest to notice, and which requires more conscious attention?

As you train your attention to see what is already abundant, your brain collects new proof. The more proof you see, the easier it becomes to live from the truth: you are already surrounded by more than enough. And it is from that state that money flows to you.

Chapter 11

Embodying Gratitude

GRATITUDE IS MORE than a nice thought or a fleeting feeling.

It is a **state of being**—a lens through which you experience the world. When you consciously embody gratitude, you amplify abundance in every area of life: health, relationships, and money.

Gratitude shifts your focus from lack to presence. It rewires your inner dialogue and creates a magnetic pull toward the life you want.

Health: Gratitude in Motion

Your body is a miracle. Every heartbeat, every breath, every movement is a gift.

- **Exercise with awareness:** Instead of pushing through fatigue or focusing on what's "wrong," notice what your body *can* do.
- Feel gratitude for strength, flexibility, and vitality.

- Even small movements—stretching, walking, or simply standing—can be infused with appreciation for the intelligence and resilience of your body.

When you embody gratitude in health, your energy shifts, your body responds positively, and the experience of wellness becomes effortless and enjoyable.

Relationships: Gratitude in Connection

Every person in your life offers opportunities for love, appreciation, and growth.

- **Interact with awareness:** Before speaking or reacting, pause to feel appreciation for the people around you.
- Express gratitude for your partner, friends, family, or colleagues—even for small gestures.
- Notice how giving gratitude freely does not deplete you; it expands connection and opens the flow of love.

Gratitude transforms ordinary interactions into moments of joy and deepens relationships naturally.

Money: Gratitude in Spending and Receiving

Money is energy, and gratitude is the amplifier.

- **Spend and receive with awareness:** Before spending or receiving money, pause and feel appreciation for its presence and utility.
- Recognize how money enables freedom, choice, and the ability to create experiences.
- Notice abundance already around you—objects, opportunities, and conveniences—and express gratitude for them. Even the electricity that we take for granted is something that gives us so much abundance and comfort. Notice the abundance in what we often take for granted.
- When spending money, feel gratitude for being able to buy something or pay a utility bill. Instead of feeling there is not enough, which creates anxiety and more of not enoughness, feel gratitude, thank you universe for supporting me to have this experience and/or enjoy these utilities.

Gratitude changes your financial vibration. You stop chasing or fearing money and instead align with the flow of prosperity.

Gratitude as a Daily Practice

1. **Morning Alignment:** Begin the day by expressing gratitude for health, relationships, and financial resources.
2. **In-the-Moment Awareness:** During exercise, interactions, or spending, consciously feel and embody gratitude.
3. **Evening Reflection:** Journal moments when gratitude amplified your experience or shifted your energy.

The Ripple Effect

Gratitude is not just a personal practice—it transforms your world.

- When you feel grateful for your body, it responds with more vitality.
- When you feel grateful for others, relationships deepen and flow.
- When you feel grateful for money, abundance appears more clearly.

Gratitude reinforces the inverse of limiting beliefs: the more you notice and embody what is already abundant, the more life mirrors that reality back to you.

Reflection & Practice: Chapter 11: Embodying Gratitude

1. Morning Gratitude Alignment

Each morning, take 3–5 minutes to consciously feel gratitude in all three areas:

Health:

- Thank your body for its strength, vitality, and the miracle of movement.
- Notice any part of your body functioning effortlessly.

Relationships:

- Express gratitude for at least one person in your life.
- Acknowledge their presence, support, or love.

Money:

- Appreciate the abundance already present—objects, resources, opportunities, or financial flows.
- Recognize how money enables freedom and choice.

Write a short note for each area in a journal.

2. Gratitude in Action

Throughout the day, intentionally embody gratitude in real-life moments:

Health:

- o During exercise, stretching, or walking, feel appreciation for what your body can do.
- o Notice how this changes your energy and performance.

Relationships:

- o Before interacting with someone, pause and feel gratitude for their presence.
- o Express appreciation openly, whether verbally or silently.

Money:

- o Before spending or receiving money, consciously feel gratitude for its availability and use.
- o Notice how this shifts your relationship with money.

3. Evening Reflection

At the end of the day, journal these prompts:

- o What moments of gratitude did I consciously notice in health, relationships, and money?
- o How did expressing gratitude influence my energy, actions, or experiences?
- o Which area felt easiest to embody gratitude, and which requires more attention?

4. Gratitude Expansion Exercise

- Pick one challenging situation in any area (body, relationship, or money).
- Ask yourself: *"What can I appreciate about this right now?"*
- Notice the shift in perception or energy when you find even a small aspect to be grateful for.

5. Weekly Integration Prompt

- Reflect on the cumulative effect of your gratitude practice over the week.
- Ask: *"How has embodying gratitude changed what I notice in life? What abundance has appeared that I previously overlooked?"*

By embodying gratitude, you shift from chasing what is missing to celebrating what already exists. And what you celebrate expands. Gratitude is the bridge between the life you live now and the life already waiting for you.

Chapter 12

Boundaries: The Gateway to True Abundance

MANY PEOPLE THINK abundance is about saying *yes* to everything. But true abundance is not found in overextending, overgiving, or overcommitting. In fact, the inability to set boundaries is often the hidden reason people struggle to experience sustainable success, health, and love.

Boundaries are not walls. They are expressions of clarity, self-worth, and trust. They say:

- *"This is where I choose to give."*
- *"This is where I choose to retract my energy."*
- *"This is what feels expansive, and this is what does not."*

Without boundaries, love becomes conditional, giving turns into resentment, and success feels unsafe.

The Myth of Overgiving

Many of us were taught that in order to receive love or approval, we must give endlessly:

- Saying yes to every request.
- Suppressing our true desires to keep others happy.
- Believing that sacrifice equals worth.

But overgiving does not create love — it creates exhaustion, resentment, and fear of success. Deep down, if you fear that more success or abundance will only mean *more demands* and *more responsibility*, you will unconsciously push it away.

The Power of Clean Communication

True boundaries are not about anger or withdrawal. They are about **clean, loving communication**:

- Saying "no" when something doesn't feel aligned.
- Saying "yes" with joy, instead of obligation.
- Speaking honestly without fear of losing love.

When you communicate from this place, you stop leaking energy. You stop living for approval. And you open space for abundance to enter.

Freedom in the Word "No"

Every time you say *no* to what does not feel enjoyable or expansive to you, you are saying *yes* to what excites you, what is actually meant for you.

- In health, this may look like saying no to toxic foods, habits, or burnout — and yes to rest, movement, and vitality.
- In relationships, it may look like saying no to conditional love — and yes to mutual respect and authentic connection.
- With money, it may look like saying no to projects that drain you — and yes to aligned opportunities that expand you.

Your "no" clears the space for your true "yes."

Story: The Garden Without a Fence

Imagine you have a lush, beautiful garden. The soil is rich, the flowers are blooming, and the fruit trees are heavy with abundance.

But there is no fence. No gate. No boundary.

At first, you welcome everyone who wanders through. They pick fruit, they trample flowers, they take what they need. You say nothing because you want to be kind. But over time, the garden grows depleted. The soil becomes compacted, the flowers stop blooming, and you begin to resent the very people you once welcomed.

Now imagine building a simple fence with a welcoming gate. Not a wall — just a clear boundary. You choose when to open the gate and when to close it. You decide who enters, and under what conditions. The soil is protected, the plants flourish, and the garden becomes even more abundant. And when you share its fruit, it's from a place of joy, not exhaustion.

Your energy is the garden. Without boundaries, your vitality, love, and creativity get trampled. With boundaries, your garden thrives, and what you share is sustainable, nourishing, and abundant.

Reflection & Practice: Chapter 12: Boundaries - The Gateway to True Abundance

1. Audit Your Yeses

Write down three areas where you regularly say yes when you really want to say no. Ask: *What am I afraid of losing if I say no?*

2. Small, Loving No

Practice saying no in a low-stakes situation today. Keep your tone kind and clean: *"Thank you, but I'm not available for that."* Notice how freeing it feels.

3. Body Check

Before saying yes, pause and check your body. Do you feel open, excited, expanded — or tense, heavy, and contracted? Let your body guide you.

4. Affirmation of Safety

Repeat daily: *"It is safe to say no. I do not lose love when I honour my truth."*

Boundaries are not restrictions. They are the foundation of freedom. Without them, success feels like a burden. With them, success becomes light, joyful, and sustainable.

When you honour your limits and set clear boundaries, something remarkable happens: you can give more freely, and receive more openly. Your "yes" carries joy, not obligation, and your "no" carries confidence, not fear. This clarity naturally opens the way to a deeper truth: the capacity to give and receive love is the same capacity to give and receive money. The boundaries you establish are not walls — they are the channels through which appreciation, generosity, and abundance flow effortlessly. As you move into the next chapter, you will explore how this flow works in practice, and how opening your hands in one area strengthens your ability to receive in the other.

By practicing this consciously, you step into a life where abundance — in love, in money, in all areas — is not just possible, it becomes inevitable.

Chapter 13

The Shared Capacity to Give and Receive (Love–Money Capacity)

AT THE DEEPEST LEVEL, love and money are not separate. They may look different on the surface, but both are expressions of **exchange, trust, and openness**.

The way you allow yourself to give and receive love is mirrored in the way you give and receive money. If you resist love, you likely resist financial flow. If you fear running out of money, you may also fear running out of affection or appreciation.

Both are governed by the same underlying capacity: your ability to open, trust, and let flow what is naturally meant to circulate.

The Closed Hand

When your beliefs are rooted in fear or scarcity, you close your hand.

- With love, that might mean holding back affection, not trusting others, or feeling unworthy of being cherished.
- With money, that might mean clinging, hoarding, or fearing loss.

A closed hand cannot give—and it also cannot receive.

The Open Hand

When your beliefs shift to abundance and flow, your hand opens.

- With love, this shows up as freely expressing kindness, appreciation, and affection without fearing you'll be depleted.
- With money, this shows up as spending, investing, and giving with trust that circulation only brings more back to you.

The open hand is not careless—it's receptive. It knows that love and money flow through you, not from you, and that both multiply when shared.

The Root Belief: Worthiness

The bridge between love and money is **worthiness**.

- If you believe you are worthy of love, you allow yourself to receive it.

- If you believe you are worthy of abundance, you allow yourself to receive money with the same ease.

Worthiness is the soil. Love and money are the fruits that grow from it.

Illustration: The River of Love and Money

Imagine standing by a wide, flowing river. The current is steady, endless, alive.

This river represents the flow of life itself—the circulation of love, money, health, and energy. The water is always moving, always replenishing itself.

Now imagine two people on opposite banks.

The first stands with a closed jar, dipping it into the water. They scoop some up, but the jar is sealed tight, afraid of losing a drop. The water inside becomes stagnant, cloudy, and lifeless. Eventually, it evaporates, leaving nothing.

The second person stands with open hands. They let the water flow through their fingers, cupping what they need, drinking deeply, and allowing the rest to return to the current. They never worry about running out, because they trust the river's endless source.

Love and money are like this river. When we cling tightly, fearing loss, we stagnate. When we open, trust, and allow flow, we are always nourished, always replenished.

The truth is: you are not the source of love or money. You are the receiver and giver, the vessel through which the river flows. The more open you are, the more fully you experience its abundance.

Reflection & Practice: Chapter 13: The Shared Capacity to Give and Receive

1. Mirror Journal: Love & Money

Take a notebook and divide it into two columns: **Love | Money**. For each column, write:

- How you **give** freely.
- How you **receive**.

Notice patterns. Are you generous in love but resist receiving? Do you freely spend money but feel uncomfortable accepting gifts?

Journal: What similarities do I notice between the way I handle love and the way I handle money?

Examples: Do I give freely but struggle to receive? Do I withhold because I fear running out? Do I overgive my energy to others, without concern for my well-being?

2. Opening Exercise

Pick one small act of giving or receiving today in both areas:

- Love: Give a genuine compliment, hug, or expression of appreciation.
- Money: Accept a gift, tip generously, or spend intentionally on something joyful.

As you do this, silently affirm: "*The more I give, the more I receive. Love and abundance flow easily through me.*"

3. Check Your Beliefs

Ask yourself: "What fear arises when I give? What fear arises when I receive?"

Journal any limiting beliefs that surface (e.g., "If I receive love, I'll be vulnerable," or "If I accept money, I'll lose control." "if I am successful, I will have to say no to people wanting something from me").

Write their inverse: "*I am safe to give and receive love. I am safe to give and receive money.*"

Give a small, intentional gift—this could be money, time, or a heartfelt expression of love.

Give yourself a gift of appreciation from yourself to yourself: a spa day, a nice evening out, a piece of clothing, flowers, etc.

As you give, say internally: *"This multiplies as it flows."*

Notice what feelings or beliefs surface.

4. Visualization: The Flowing Hands

Close your eyes. Imagine holding both love and money in your hands.

Picture your hands opening slowly, letting both flow freely through you and back into the world.

Feel the joy, ease, and trust in this circulation.

Repeat daily:

- *"As I open to love, I open to abundance."*
- *"My capacity to receive expands with my willingness to give."*

5. Daily Alignment Check

Each morning or evening, reflect:

- Where did I resist giving or receiving today?
- Where did I overgive/overwork today?
- Where did I allow love or abundance to flow effortlessly?

Note shifts, no matter how small. Over time, this builds a habit of noticing the flow rather than scarcity.

By recognizing that love and money are two sides of the same flow, you reclaim your innate openness. Every time you open your heart to love, you expand your ability to welcome financial abundance. And every time you allow money to flow, you affirm your capacity to receive love.

Conclusion

Your Life, Aligned

AS YOU CONTINUE to honour your boundaries and allow abundance to flow freely in love, money, and life itself, you create a foundation for alignment. The energy you cultivate through clarity, self-care, and conscious giving and receiving prepares you to fully integrate all the practices in this book.

You've now explored the way beliefs shape every corner of your life—health, relationships, money, and inner talk—and learned how to:

- Unsubscribe from limiting beliefs that no longer serve you.
- Notice the abundance that is already present everywhere.
- Embody gratitude to amplify life's natural flow.
- Live the inverse of scarcity, struggle, and self-doubt.

The key to all of this is simple: your inner world creates your outer world. The stories you tell yourself, the beliefs you carry, and the thoughts you repeat are reflected back at you in the form of your actual life.

Your Invitation

Now it's time to step fully into your power.

- **Notice:** Become aware of the thoughts, beliefs, and stories that run your life.
- **Unsubscribe:** Release the beliefs that limit you in health, love, and wealth.
- **Shift your focus:** Look for evidence of abundance and proof of the inverse.
- **Embody gratitude:** Infuse every action and interaction with appreciation.
- **Live the inverse:** Align your energy with the truth that vitality, love, and abundance are your natural state.

When you do this consistently, change is no longer a struggle. Life begins to flow effortlessly, mirroring the freedom, abundance, and joy you cultivate within.

A Final Thought

Transformation is not about doing more. It's about being differently.

- Being aligned.
- Being aware.
- Being grateful.
- Being open to the abundance that surrounds you.

Every step you take in awareness, every thought you consciously choose, every moment of gratitude, is a seed. Water these seeds, and your life will flourish beyond what you thought possible. You are not waiting for change—you are already the person who embodies it. The proof of your new life is already here, appearing in every breath, every connection, and every opportunity that surrounds you.

Boundaries protect your flow.

Safety and Love open your hands.

Giving and receiving are one.

Love circulates. Money circulates. Life circulates.

Notice the abundance already here.

Embody gratitude in every breath, every connection, every choice.

You are already aligned. You are already abundant. You are already whole.

If this book has resonated with you, I want you to know you are not alone. I'm Julie Cloutier, a Wealth Consciousness Mentor, and I have spent years helping people uncover the beliefs that quietly shape their lives—and guiding them to step fully into their true potential.

If you feel called to go deeper:

- Explore your unconscious beliefs.
- Expand your emotional intelligence.
- Reclaim your true identity.
- Embody your highest potential effortlessly.

My work includes **Wealth Codes Embodied,** an evergreen 6-month immersion in wealth energetic embodiment, and **Wealth Codes Accelerator**, an exclusive 6-week private mentorship for those ready to unlock their next level of wealth and freedom.

To learn more or apply, visit www.juliecloutier.com

Or email me at hello@juliecloutier.com.

Thank you for opening your heart to this book. May it guide you back to the freedom, abundance, and joy that were never lost—only waiting to be remembered.

With love and infinite abundance,

Julie Cloutier

Wealth Activator

Acknowledgments

THIS BOOK IS THE result of curiosity, love, and the courage to question everything I thought I knew.

To my partner, who asked the questions that led me to the answers—thank you for being my mirror, my guide, and my companion on this journey from struggle to freedom.

To my teachers, students, clients, mentors, colleagues, friends, and family—thank you for your wisdom, your support, and your unwavering belief in the power of transformation.

In truth, expansion is possible on our own, but it becomes magnified when others choose to expand too. Every soul who has crossed my path has reflected a new layer of awareness back to me—and for that, I am endlessly grateful.

I'm deeply grateful to Robert Rugg, who opened the door for me to the world of writing and publishing—and with whom I had the joy of co-authoring my very first book, *Effortless Abundance: The Art of Thriving Without Struggle*. Robert, I always knew I had a book within me, but you opened the path that allowed it to come through with ease.

Deep gratitude as well to Kathryn Galán of Wynnpix Productions —your work is impeccable, your care evident. And to Pixel Studios, thank you for your beautiful contribution to this book's cover design.

And finally, to you, dear reader—thank you for opening yourself to this work. May it remind you that the life you desire isn't something to be created—it already exists, ready for you to claim.

About the Author

JULIE CLOUTIER is a transformational mentor and creator of *The Wealth Activation Movement*™ — a global call to rise beyond fear, lack, and striving, and return to the natural state of wealth that already lives within.

Through her groundbreaking work in wealth consciousness and energetic mastery, she guides leaders, visionaries, and creators to dissolve scarcity patterns and embody effortless prosperity.

With a unique blend of spiritual depth and practical clarity, Julie helps her clients return to their natural state of abundance — where ease replaces striving, and wealth becomes a reflection of being more of who they truly are.

Books by Julie Cloutier

Effortless Abundance: The Art of Thriving without Struggle (with Robert Rugg). Also available on Audible.

The Belief Detox: Stop Believing, Start Living

Connect with Julie via:

YouTube channel @juliecloutierchannel

Website: www.juliecloutier.com

Email at hello@juliecloutier.com

Printed in Dunstable, United Kingdom

76454559R00068